D0031176

STUDIO PRESS

Printed Under License ©2017 Emotional Rescue
www.emotional-rescue.com
Published by Studio Press
An imprint of Kings Road Publishing. Part of Bonnier Publishing
The Plaza, 535 King's Road, London, SW10 0SZ

www.bonnierpublishing.co.uk

Printed in Italy   10 9 8 7 6 5 4 3 2 1

The Wit & Wisdom of
THE HUSBAND

As far as he was concerned, it was called a 'Remote' because of the chance of ever getting the opportunity to use it!

O n their road trip from London to Brighton, he finally stopped to ask directions but he couldn't understand a word the bloke in the kilt said.

hen it came to arguing, they always compromised... he admits he'd been wrong and his wife agreed with him.

He is astonished! His wife asked him to do the washing up again, and he had to remind her that he'd done it twice already, once in 1993 and again in 1995!

hat evening, his wife asked him to do that thing that all men fear and dread — fetch her some tampons from the chemist.

Few things amused him quite so much as watching the wife trying to reverse park the car!

"ven... O... V... E... N!" she repeated as she tried to teach him the names of all the kitchen appliances.

He had what is considered to be the best labour saving device in the world... it was called 'A Wife'.

He had been waiting a 'little while' for his wife to get ready to go out.

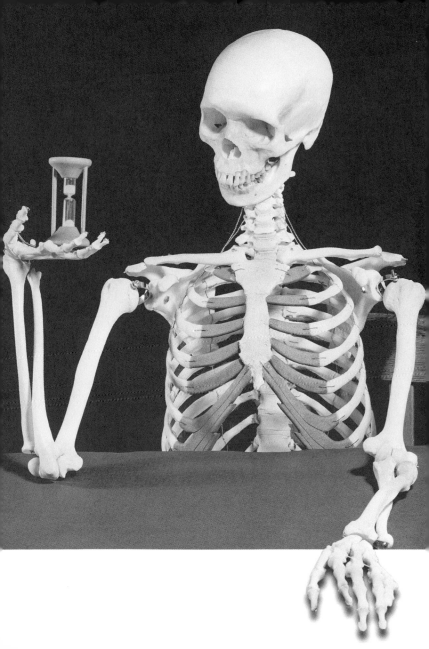

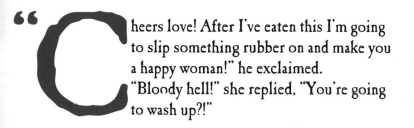

"Cheers love! After I've eaten this I'm going to slip something rubber on and make you a happy woman!" he exclaimed.
"Bloody hell!" she replied, "You're going to wash up?!"

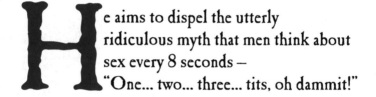

He aims to dispel the utterly ridiculous myth that men think about sex every 8 seconds –
"One... two... three... tits, oh dammit!"

his was to be the most romantic poem ever put to paper. He cast his inhibitions to the wind, and began to commit his very heart and soul to the page. *'Dear Bouncytits...'*

Her dreams of romance were shattered when her husband joined her for a sh*t and a shave.

He was clueless about the kitchen, he thought 'loading the dishwasher' meant getting his wife drunk.

He learns to never, *ever* tell his wife that 'Strictly Come Dancing' is crap!

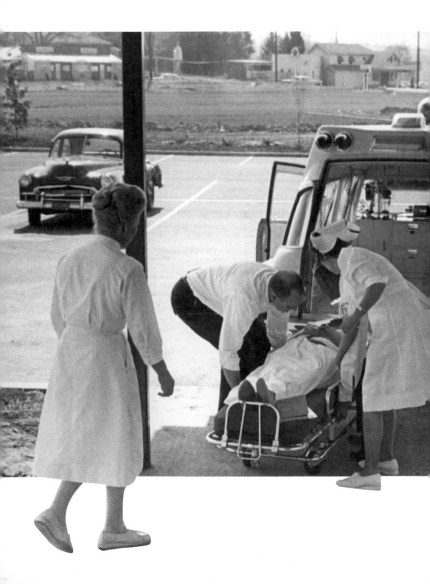

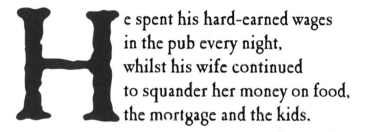

He spent his hard-earned wages
in the pub every night,
whilst his wife continued
to squander her money on food,
the mortgage and the kids.

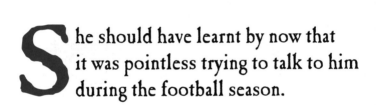

She should have learnt by now that it was pointless trying to talk to him during the football season.

He was determined to find his wife's G spot, but didn't know what postcode to put in the satnav.

hile he did his best to appear completely captivated by everything his wife was saying, he was mentally planning his next golfing holiday.

ecorating the front room was much more important to him than watching the football. Why...?
Because his wife had told him it was!

He finally accepts that if at first you don't succeed, try doing it how your wife told you in the first place.

In an act of sweet revenge, he drags his wife around a load of pubs only to go back to the very first one he went in to buy a pint.

irst the dishwasher, then the washing machine, followed by the hoover and the lawnmower. How on earth was he supposed to concentrate on reading the newspaper when his wife insisted on making so much noise?

"**I** really love you!" he said.
"Is that the beer talking?" she asked.
"No, that's me talking to the beer!"